AFTERTHOUGHTS

A Collection

By

Tony Dawson

'For Janet'

Contents

Embers

Three years old,
I'm in a garden
in the middle of Rectory Square.

The embers in remembers
keep the memory warm.

Then, escape from the Blitz
in a taxi, lit by flares
snagged on bombed-out buildings.

For the embers in remembers
are stirred by the war in warm.

Our new house is quite empty,
except for a black grate;
red brick's replaced by pebbledash.

The embers in remembers
have still not turned to ash.

My mother's eyes
and cheeks are glowing.
Now, she is content.

Alas, the embers in remembers
are almost spent:

the Junkers drone above again,
relief soon turns to fear.
Huddled by the staircase,

the embers in remembers
recall her warm embrace.

Rita

Calderón de la Barca likened
life to a form of madness,
an illusion, an insubstantial shadow,
a fiction, since all of life's a dream
and dreams themselves are dreams.
This ontological-cum-epistemological
conundrum is a tough one, to say the least.
But is nothing real? Are you and I
simply living our particular dream?

Rita was the apple of my mother's eye
and also mine. She was the perfect
big sister: bright, beautiful, and caring.
She coddled me when I was young,
cuddled me during air raids
and helped me with my homework.
From early on, everyone knew
that she would be the first
in our family to go to university.
She studied medicine at Edinburgh
and eventually became
a renowned epidemiologist.
How I miss her now!
. . . .
When I'm alone with my thoughts,
these are my idle imaginings
of Rita's Calderonian dream life.
In reality, I have only ever seen
a blurred black and white photo

of her, as a baby, held aloft
for the camera by my adoring mother.
For the sad truth is that my sister
broke our parents' hearts
by dying suddenly, in her cot,
when she was three months old.

Pater Noster

I was abroad when I heard the news:
my father had had a stroke!
Apparently, his brain had blown a fuse,
maybe because he liked to smoke
and, when younger, used to booze:
a typical working-class bloke.

It was an unexpected shock to me.
He really seemed too tough to die,
the hardest man who'd worked the quay,
a "don't-mess-with-me" kind of guy.
I'm sure that few would disagree
with me. *Even so, I did not cry.*

I'd felt his heavy hand as a child.
His sharp tongue could also wound
especially when he was riled.
It seemed as though he was doomed
to lose control. Later we'd be reconciled,
and normal life would be resumed.

....

I went to see him when I returned.
The contrast with the man I knew
came as the greatest shock: he'd turned
to skin and bone. This wasn't the Hugh
of old. Gone was that compact physique
of sinewed muscle, with arms like Popeye.
His chances of recovery looked bleak

but I still couldn't bring myself to cry.
His body was shrunken and twisted,
that tongue, 'an instrument now stringless'.
With one arm hanging useless, he listed
left, his sharp tongue now stingless.
From the corner of his mouth, drool
oozed out and trickled down his chin.
How ironic that destiny had made a fool
of such a man, one as tough as him.

Two months later my brother rang
to tell me our father had died.
However, I still didn't feel a pang
of remorse. *I remained resolutely dry-eyed.*

Family Funeral 1

A couple of months after our father's stroke,
my brother rang when I was in bed.
His voice was triumphant as he spoke.
He was dying to tell me our father was dead!
"He died in my arms," he crowed down the phone
(A pietà vision of Bob holding Dad!),
his tone implying that I should have known.
"Why ring me at midnight?" I groaned, "Are you mad?"
"Who else would I ring, if not you, dude?"
he retorted, missing the point by a mile.
This brief exchange was the start of our feud
that lasted for decades because that was his style.
I drove down from Liverpool in the northwest.
The crematorium parlour was all plastic and chromium
with a handful of mourners in the Chapel of Rest.
The deacon delivered an anodyne encomium
for the deceased all dressed in his Sunday best.
Then, to piped music, but with no other rites
the corpse was welcomed to its simulacrum of Hell
to incinerate his bones, his liver, and lights.
Turning to me my brother said, "So, that went off well!"
"You're joking", I cried. "I thought it was dire!"
The living then filed into the room next door.
Some wit enquired if the wick was lit by a friar,
as the rest of us feigned gloom and gazed at the floor.
The ashes were handed in an urn to my brother
and Dad's name inscribed in the Book of Remembrance.
Much the same thing had happened to our mother
but at least, in her case, there was a semblance

of sincerity in the feelings of those who were there.
She would have lived longer if life had been fair.
The early arrivals at the wake took their pick
of Dad's stuff, though most of it was tat.
I joked lamely about them being so quick
in the home of the dead, but who understood that?
The atmosphere at the wake was unbearably tense,
relations with my brother were strained.
He seemed to have taken serious offence
at something that was never explained.
At the end of the wake, as they say,
I made my excuses and left.
It would have been normal on such a day
for the bereaved to be feeling bereft.
A linguistic quirk had put "fun" in funeral,
yet it never appeared in this case.
Dad became just another numeral
in the Book of Remembrance, the only trace
anywhere that he'd ever existed.
(Meanwhile, the feud with my brother persisted.)

Family Funeral 2

Twenty years later he rang me again
suggesting we stopped playing silly buggers.
By then, of course, I was living in Spain;
I agreed we should start behaving like brothers.
I was touched he had decided to ring
and looked forward to seeing him once more.
I invited him over the following spring.
He was so happy we'd ended our 'war'.
But, during that year he became unwell,
complaining of pains in his chest.
How ill he'd become I was unable to tell
until he received the result of a test.
It turned out that he had an unusual cancer
which was inoperable and the treatment expensive,
The oncologists, it seemed, had no other answer.
Nonetheless, my brother put on a brave face.
The hospital care was thorough and intensive,
yet he had no choice but to brace
himself for the fact his carcinoma was rare.
As chemo was proving to be ineffective,
he was put into palliative care.
A death sentence certainly puts life in perspective.
I kept ringing the hospice utterly distraught,
while he sobbed down the phone at the prospect of dying.
My words were a jumble, a discourse so fraught
for I couldn't cope with the fact he was crying.
In a matter of weeks he wasted away.
The futile years of our quarrel were what I most rued.
His wife was heartbroken, needless to say,
while Atropos mocked at our family feud.

Brief Bio

First a son and
instant brother;
next a husband,
father, lover;
a judoka,
joker, smoker;
violent, gentle,
often gracious;
splendid host,
too flirtatious,
agile wit,
sometimes tasteless.

Another man
without a plan
who gave life
and living it
so little thought,
he was surprised
when painful Death
cut him off
still in his prime.
A sharp reminder:
life is short.

Tailgating Time

I've been moving steadily through life
for more than eighty years now,
occasionally breaking the speed limit,
in my youth, of course, only to slow down
later, dawdling, allowing time to pass.
But time doesn't really *pass* anyone.
It's a myth. It's trying to catch you up,
drawing inexorably closer and closer.
Suddenly, Andy Marvell's wingèd chariot
has become a tailgating pickup truck
like the type you see in the movies
driven by some redneck intent on
pushing me off the road into the ditch.
Why does Time insist on harassing the old?

Lithuanian Cat's Cradle

Cats are mysterious, or so people claim
and you were as exotic as they came.
Being a 'Siamese' pussy
of Lithuanian extraction
certainly added to the attraction:
isosceles face—high cheekbones, pointy chin—
arch smile; (I was now sucked in);
and eyes with mischievous epicanthic folds…
"Boxer's eyes", you called them.
They certainly knocked me cold!
And finally the *frisson* in your name,
Nijole…

You had a way of sitting, legs crossed,
knees wide apart, provocatively
offering your love triangle to me—
a cat's cradle for the lost.
And how you rocked me!
I could almost hear you purring
as my loins were stirring.
Yes, you were a real pussycat!

You had a dancer's seductive grace,
and when you sang: 'The first time ever I saw your face…'
I was caught, snagged in your claws like a ball of wool.
Of course, you were making a fool
of me while I was giving you my trust.
I was being out-manoeuvred

as you hoovered
up my lust.

You were a feral lover,
a screamer, sublime.
I thought 'our steps would always rhyme'
but you were a predator
and when a likelier prey came on the scene
you spat me out, discarded and half-chewed,
then 'devoured' the terminally subdued
Dr Crisp. You liked your men well done.

Chance Encounter (1990)

Though I haven't travelled far,
I stop in el Rocío at a bar
to have a snack.
And there you are,
leaning back in a chair
beneath the awning,
on the terrace.

Despite the chill in the air
(it's early spring and mid-morning)
you're lightly clad in chinos
and a faded red top
that timidly suggests
your breasts.

Your slender arms are bare,
while your short hair,
tousled and awry,
highlights your youthful face.

With eyes half-closed
against the sun,
you turn away from me.
(Perhaps you're shy
and wish to shun
this stranger's visual embrace.)

Yet your sun-drenched lips,
swollen with a thousand

unused kisses,
are parted in what seems to me
a knowing smile…

I'm convinced this is an invitation
to start a conversation, so I try.
You are polite, but distant,
my flight of fantasy
crashing in an instant
as again you turn away.

Now, awkward, and embarrassed
I don't know what to say.
Meanwhile, at another table
an old man wearing shades
is staring. He can't grasp
the meaning of this scene we're playing —
any more than I can now
after nearly three decades...

Love's a Laugh

"La capacité de rire ensemble, voilà ce qu'est l'amour"
Françoise Sagan.

"Love's the ability to laugh together,
says the author of *Bonjour Tristesse*,
without a hint of irony…", my wife scoffed.
"Maybe she's implying she never loved…
After all, laughter therapy's one thing
but laughing your way through life's
a tall order," I replied, with a smile.
"What about pessimists? Aren't they allowed
to be gloomy and still *love*?" she growled.
"It's true," I said, "some people *love*
being miserable. They *love* to wallow."
"But one wallow doesn't make a depression,
unless you're a water buffalo," she quipped.
"Is that supposed to make me laugh?" I asked.
"If so, I'm not so sure we love each other!"

Octave for Janet

Spring and summer blossoms populated
our family tree that stood so straight and tall.
Then the blossoms gradually faded into fall
bringing the fruit that we so eagerly awaited.
When our winter hesitated and finally never
came, apparently because of climate change,
our blossoms bloomed and flourished once again.
An Indian summer in which to bask forever.

How Do I Love You? Let Me Count the Ways

I love you standing up or lying down,
I love your smile and when you frown.
I love to taste your Carly Simon lips
I love the sway of your shapely hips.
I love the throaty gurgle of your laughter
when I amuse you, and especially after,
when you reward me with the warmest hug.
I love curling up with you in bed, so snug.
You make my declining years content,
the keeper of a flame that's not yet spent.
If only we could start our journey once again,
further back from where we then were able,
say fourteen years before our idyll here in Spain
began to turn our fruitful romance into fable...

In a Rut

At dawn, a Yorkshire bar was emptying out.
Some boisterous young lads were laiking about,
ogling and braying at provocative lasses
prancing around and showing their asses.

In nearby woodland, fallow deer formed a lek,
a rutting display by young bucks at the beck
and call of oestrous does that decided the fate
of each of the males as they selected a mate.

Out in the carpark, each of the lasses decided the fate
of each lad, driving off in a taxi with her chosen mate.

Each doe in the woodland paired off with a buck
and after a brief chase was cornered and ... mounted.

In a Rut includes a northern English dialect word 'laiking'.
The Yorkshire dialect word 'laik' derives directly from the Swedish
word 'lek' meaning 'play' or 'game'. In the context of deer rutting,
it means a small group of male deer that put on a ritual perfor-
mance for the benefit of oestrous hinds that come looking for a
mate. Other interesting linguistic points are 1) that the Danish equiva-
lent of 'lek' is 'leg', which forms part of the word Lego (leg + godt)
meaning 'play well'; 2) 'laik' a Yorkshire dialect word has come
into the language meaning 'playing (about) or 'messing about' be-
cause after the Viking invasion of Britain that area together with a
large part of northern England was in the Danelaw and Viking words
came into the language.

Attempted Suicide

"I'm going to commit suicide this afternoon," he said.
"There's enough in the bank for you to live on."
"Hell, I don't want you hanging around, especially dead,"
she retorted, "and I don't fancy bumping into carrion!"
"I could shoot myself if you prefer. I'll buy a gun."
"You can't do that. There'll be blood all over the walls!"
she growled. "Why not line the room with plastic for a dry run?"
he suggested. "It will still look like bloody Niagara Falls!"
she shot back. "Well, I could try strychnine or cyanide,"
he muttered under his breath. "What if the dog licked your face?"
she screamed, aghast, "and died? You're so selfish," she cried.
"I can't think of everything. Keep the dog outside, just in case.
How about if I slash my wrists while lying in the bath?"
"Apart from the fact that you *lie* no matter where you are,
it doesn't cross your mind *I'll* have to use it later, you psychopath!
Just go and drink yourself to death in the nearest bar!"
"Drink makes me ill. Why don't you simply nag me to death?"
"Because that would be murder, not suicide, my dear.
Much as I'd like to see you draw your last breath,
I don't want to end up inside and hear you cheer
from the great beyond. I'd rather enjoy your savings."
"I think we've reached an impasse," said he, "Let's talk
about it another day." "OK, now that you've stopped your ravings,
we'll put the rope, poison, and plastic away, and go for a walk."

Hidden meanings

'Ire' lurks in your desire
while your eyes conceal a 'yes'
from everyone but me.

I also 'hear' your heartbeat
and the 'ask' hidden by the mask
that keeps the virus at bay.

You are my *touch*stone, yet out of reach.
My 'urge' is purged, your 'lips' eclipsed
until such time as COVID dies.

Graffiti: Wall to Wall Wisdom

Poetry is eternal graffiti written in the heart of everyone,
Lawrence Ferlinghetti

Skins Rule, O.K.?
Lunacy drools, O.K.?
Dyslexia lures, K.O.?
Heisenberg's Uncertainty
Principle Rules perhaps, O.K.?
Absolute Zero Rules, O.K.?
French Fishers Rule, Au Quai?
Moby Dick is not a disease.
You are what you eat.
"I've just eaten Einstein"
said the cannibal,
"making me a genius, O.K.?"
Paul Foot, a legend in his own time.

Online Poetry Magazines: O.P.M. for Would-be Coleridges?

An O.P.M beckons…
a site for sore I's
where tortured egos
can parade their angst;
an existential haven
for souls in torment,
adrift in a sea of doubt,
to moor their rafts of despair…
and then repair
to the supermarket
before the milk's sold out.

But let's not forget that
O.P.M.'s the drug of choice
for the 'poets of ideas'.
They think its potent effect
gives them a 'voice',
the illusion that they
'really do have
something to say'…

And O.P.M. works miracles
for the bard who waxes lyrical
about 'how the words are stuck'.
But if he's really out of luck,
frustrated with his lot,
hit the wall, lost the plot,
finds himself in thrall

because the words no longer run amok
and he's suffering from writer's block…
just blame the man from Porlock!

Maradona Meets His Maker

At last, the World Cup's little faker
shuffled off to meet his Maker.
Soccer's odious little midget
who loved to flick his middle digit
at losers on the field of play
has finally passed away.
Whether he was buried or was burned
his reputation's now been *urned*!

So, let's *not* praise dear Maradona,
Argentina's prima donna,
the man who was a walking arsehole.
The "hand of God" that scored *that* goal,
and made the beautiful game a farce,
also wiped Diego's arse,
then beat the women in his life,
whether girlfriends or his wife.

Good riddance to the cheating sod.
At least, in the end he didn't linger
and if he saw the hand of God
I hope he got the middle finger!

An App for Ancient Swingers

If you're over 80 and still a little skittish,
then our app's designed especially for you…
We've ironed out all the wrinkles and furthermore it's British.
The demand's been overwhelming, so hurry, join the queue!
If your aging body's up to it and you are into mating.
Roll up, roll up you oldies for the app called Carbon Dating!

Joan of Arc or the Law of Unintended Consequences

Joan of Arc
cried, "It's got dark.
Let's light up the sky!"
So, a passing friar
set her on fire
and now we all know why…

Poetry by design

True poetry's designer language,
the Lamborghini of the written word.
It's a fugue by Shostakovich,
sounds that simply must be heard.
It's the Bauhaus of the printed page.
Timeless, like a Rolex fake,
the universal way to gauge
emotions that can make
you drunk, like the tempranillo grape.
As eye-catching as an angler's hook,
as streamlined as a dolphin's shape,
they're the words that make a book a book.
But mostly poetry's just a bit of fun
and difficult to handle, like a sticky bun!

Case Closed

A woman's torso was found
in a suitcase in a dark alley,
and her head, in a laundry bag
on the bank of the Potomac.
The arms were in a plastic bag
next to her legs, which were
tied together in a kit bag.
When questioned by the police,
the boyfriend claimed he didn't know
where she'd gone. She'd simply split.
"She was driving me nuts," he said,
 "So, I just sent her packing…"

Dead To Rights

Liam and Mick had hatched a plan.
They needed some cash for they were broke.
They used to care for an older man
who'd died that day of a massive stroke.
Liam went to collect his pension,
"for the man himself's too ill to come."
The clerk in the office paid no attention.
"He has to come. It's a tidy sum,
I'm not allowed to give it to you."
So, Liam went home to confer with Mick.
They supported the corpse—whose face was blue—
as if he were drunk. Could they pull off the trick?
Later, I heard a young woman tell
the police that "when they went for the pension,
the man in the middle looked quite unwell.
He couldn't walk, which I forgot to mention."
When one of the young men asked for payment,
The clerk in the office refused again.
"All requests have to come from the claimant."
The young men let go of the corpse to explain.
The body collapsed and dropped to the floor.
Mick and Liam both screamed in horror.
Mick turned white and Liam swore
under his breath, "Begosh and begorra!
We said he was ill and unable to come,
you could see he was poorly, just as we said.
But you insisted. See what you've done.
Our dear old friend has fallen down dead.
You'd best call the Gardai. We're going to sue.
You made him come, so his death is on you!"

Memory

"You know more than you are telling us,"
said the cop, staring at me across the table.
"We always know more than we remember,"
I replied. "Let me give you a 'for instance'.
I used to know every single name
of my mother's nine brothers and sisters
but now I can only remember two or three.
It's the old grey matter test, you see.
When someone says he forgets, it means
he doesn't remember not that he doesn't know.
So, of course I know more than I'm telling you
but it's because I don't remember. Can I go?"

I am waiting for the coronavirus to lose its crown
A pastiche of and tribute to Lawrence Ferlinghetti

I am waiting for the coronavirus
to lose its crown
and I am waiting for my sorrows
to finally drown
I am waiting for the billionaires and squillionaires
to pay their fair share
of taxes
and I wonder
if it's worth waiting
for a rebirth of anything

I am waiting
for the sugar mountain to dissolve
and disappear before the world dies
of diabetes of the hate-fuelled kind
and I am waiting
for the last tweet to sound
as the bluebird icon
turns up its toes
so that we can hear real birdsong
for a change
and I am waiting for the star-spangled banner
to ban overseas wars
so that it no longer
has to be draped over coffins
and I wonder

if there's any chance of a rebirth
of goodwill

I am waiting to revisit
my misspent youth
a trip down mammary lane
to raise my spirits
(not to mention the flesh)
and I am waiting for somebody
to clarify the Danish numbering system
for me and explain
why the Yupno tribe use their bodies
to count and not an abacus
I am also waiting
for my number to come up
hoping it will be the Yupno thirty-three

I am waiting for QAnons to be returned
to their padded cells
and I am waiting for the United States
to stop turning up trumps
and sending undesirables up Indian Creek
without a paddle
and I am waiting
for the pussy-grabbing fake president
to be punished for his Capitol sins
and I am waiting for those whose names
rhyme with Paul Anka
to be scooped up and dumped
off the coast of Florida
and hope that those who live in that state
never find what Ferlinghetti did:
the Fountain of Eternal Youth

Parody of 'I wandered lonely as a cloud'

I wandered lonely as a Proud
Boy o'er the Capitol's windowsills
When all at once I saw a crowd
Of climate-change denier shills.
Beside old Trump, I saw Ted Cruz
Whose brows were tattooed with 'confuse'.

As porcine as the Gadarene swine
On the way to meet their death,
They stretched in never-ending line
Evidently high on alt-right meth.
Ten thousand saw I at a glance
Lumbering by in Trumpian dance.

LA Christmas Present

Trying on a dress in a store
is the latest high-risk pursuit.
A cop's body cam footage
showed it all on TV:

A young man, high on drugs
(maybe), and unarmed, had been
attacking other customers.
A dozen LAPD officers
arrived, led by Rambo toting
an assault rifle. When he saw
the possible junkie at the far
end of the aisle, he fired off
three bullets in quick succession.
The third one went through the wall
of a dressing room, and hit
a teenage girl in the chest,
as she tried on a Christmas dress.
She died in her mother's arms,
Now Rambo's at home on paid leave.

In 2021, the LAPD shot
38 people; 18 of them died.
Have they beaten their record yet?
Are only trigger-happy cops
recruited? If only the girl
had tried on a bullet-proof
vest instead of a dress…
The City of Angels wouldn't have welcomed
another one, thanks to the LAPD.

The Six-Shooter

So, a pretty young teacher tried to take
a handgun from a stroppy six-year-old.
The sort of incident that could happen
anywhere in the world, right?
Well, only if you share Americans'
traditional love-affair with firearms.

I imagine the cocky little kid pulling
back, holding the gun above his head
and imitating Charlton Heston's drawl,
smirking, "From my cold dead hands".
Then, pointing the gun at the teacher,
he coolly shot her in the abdomen.

Clutching the wound in a reflex action,
she lay bleeding on the floor, calling
to the other children to flee the class.
Yet people still react with shock
at such an event, immediately dredging up
the same old tired clichés: hearts reach out,
prayers and thoughts are with those
who are suffering, guns need to be kept
out of the hands of young people...
knowing full well that this is just the latest
in an endless series of gun-related incidents
in schools and that nothing will ever change.

The Worm in the Rose

Since 1986, the rose has been
the national flower of the USA.
But just like Blake's rose, it is sick
and the worm in the rose is the NRA.

Some kids in Dadeville were shot dead
at a Sweet Sixteen birthday party.
Alabama governor, Kay Ivey, said:
"There's no place for violent crime in our state."

Yet in 2022, Ivey signed a bill into law:
no permit needed for a concealed handgun.
The NRA, always quick on the draw,
had also made sure to lobby for it.

In an ad for Ivey's re-election campaign,
the governor pulled a handgun
from her purse, as once again
she wooed her gun-friendly voters.

And only recently in a Louisville bank
A disgruntled employee carrying a rifle
shot his companions at point-blank
range, killing four and wounding more.

If some black kid knocks on your door,
the NRA says, "Stand your ground!
Teach him not to hang around:
Just use your Magnum 44!"

Prudence

If shooting children is your hobby
support the NRA's gun lobby.

My daughter Prudence is only five
and so to help her stay alive
when she goes off to school
or "to the front" and be real cool,
she packs a Browning Buck Mark
in case some psycho for a lark
decides to shoot up all the students.
He'll have to reckon with my Prudence.

End Times

The oceans are finally choked with plastic.
The poles are melting like butter in the sun.
We humans must do something drastic
or there'll be no place for us to run.

Our countries' leaders meet and cheat
and spend their time prevaricating,
with every speech a masked deceit.
For none will do what they are advocating.

Once Pandora's box was opened,
allowing the polluters to run free,
we had to bank on hope and
common sense to find the key

to lock the box or devise a plan,
beyond a useless summit meeting,
to save the world, and maybe man,
and stop the Earth from overheating.

Reviewing the problems leads to despair.
With our lives in the hands of egomaniacs,
it's more than likely we don't have a prayer.
Humanity's demise is the probable climax.

Ubi sunt qui...?

Where are the politicians of yesteryear
who had the country's wellbeing at heart?
When will new Attlees and Beveridges appear
to redistribute wealth and so make a start
by stimulating the economy and society,
to make life worth living for everyone,
banish homelessness, cuts, and anxiety
and show that life can also be fun
and full of hope, dreams, and expectation?
Where are the statesmen to achieve this?
Where are the women to rescue the nation
from those who have given the kiss
of death to our lives and our hopes?
How do we rid ourselves of so much dross,
MPs who come out with all the old tropes
and force the rest of us to bear their cross?

Sights and Sounds

An old man lay dying in his hospital bed,
hometown memories dancing through his head:

luggage on wheels being dragged over cobbles
by leggy blonde tourists with phones in their hands.
TV advertisements for watches designed
with those prone to accidents clearly in mind.
Supermarket trolleys piled high with junk
going bin to bin in search of some treasure.
Electric-powered scooters whizzing past on the path,
too close for comfort, disturbing his leisure.
Hoarse homeless voices of endless unfortunates
wheezing appeals to passing pedestrians.
The whistling sound of panpipes from the past?
A knife-grinder touting his skill in the market.
Drunken strangers disturbing the peace,
deciding it's fun to spew up on the pavement
while hurling abuse at the local police
as part of their holiday entertainment.
The plaintive *quejíos* of Flamenco singing,
the *picados* and *rasgueados* of acoustic guitars?
Signs of Sevillians determinedly wringing
emotions from life as they carouse in the bars...
His hometown memories keep coming back
until they eventually fade away, fade to black.

Fade to Black

It's not easy to "rage against the dying of the light."
It takes too much energy, now in short supply.
Why fight the final fade-out to exhaustion?
What's one supposed to do? Keep labouring on?
Continue to weave the tapestry of existence
as it unravels between arthritic fingers?
Or stoop to pick up another skein of fading life
even though standing up again is painful?

It turns out that Dylan Thomas, who coined
this rallying cry, died not from an alcoholic
"insult to the brain" caused by excessive drinking,
but from pneumonia and a dim 'celebrity' doctor,
Falkenstein, who pumped him full of morphine
having diagnosed the poet with delirium tremens,
maybe under the influence of the writer's initials...

Life on the Streets

A fairytale crone,
dressed in black
from head to toe,
leans on a walking frame
in a busy street in Seville,
holding out her hand,
an avatar of woe.
Like the melting, evil,
Witch of the West
in the Wizard of Oz,
and just as tiny,
her magic's waned.
The shoppers hurry by
as if she's invisible.

On another street
a homeless man
is hunched in the shadow
of the Church of All Saints,
a gargoyle fallen
from his perch
on the cornice.
The old lurcher,
wheezing by his side,
is just as gaunt,
no longer able
to daunt anyone.
The man's eyes are dead,

staring straight ahead,
yet registering nothing.

In the alleyway called
Loves' Passage,
which adjoins
Bitterness street—
what sardonic wit
gave them such names? —
another man is sleeping
under a grubby blanket
on a piece of foam rubber
inside a cardboard box,
perhaps dreaming of a banquet.
Passers-by steer well clear,
consumed as they are
by irrational fear.

Solidarity

Sitting in the doorway of a dilapidated library
wrapped in blankets, morning, noon, and night,
quietly reading books or offering some rosemary,
two men, in solidarity, coping with their plight:
friends who've spent long years surviving on the street.
Two homeless men both holding out their palms
like *yogis* meditating, hoping for a treat?
Or a bite to eat? No … Just brothers in alms.

Holy Man or Homeless Man?

We could see him in profile
as we walked along the street.
A baseball-capped holy man
was sitting in a doorway
on our route to the supermarket!
Bearded and hollow-cheeked,
gazing into an imagined distance,
he muttered a word or two
as we passed by with the trolley.
Was it a mantra? Or a blessing?

"What was that about peccadillos,"
I asked my wife as we walked on.
"I think he asked for a *bocadillo*"
she muttered, rolling her eyes.
So, not a holy man after all.
He was a homeless man
begging for food on the street.
I felt ashamed of myself.

On the way back, we stopped
at his niche on the step.
He sat motionless, his glassy
blue eyes staring straight ahead
as if in a trance, meditating.
He said nothing. Perplexing.
Was he in fact a holy man?
Or was he simply ignoring me

as I'd appeared to ignore him?
No doubt I deserved his disdain.

We stood facing him. His gaze
passed through us like a laser.
I held out some money for him
and it appeared an eternity
before he awoke from his trance
and realized I was offering help.
His grateful courtesy was touching.
There are so many like him in Seville.
Hope has drained from their faces
and the life from their eyes.

The End of a Reign

The Queen died and life itself stood still.
For many she'd appeared immortal.
How did she slip through the portal
of death against the people's will?

The only movement has been the pall
passing slowly through each town,
streets lined with mourners as if they all
were intimates of the wearer of the crown.

Government and politics are paralyzed,
in a state of suspended animation,
bewildered and disoriented, as they realize
the impact of her death upon the nation.

International resonance has also been profound,
the news reverberating all around the world,
and in former colonies we've heard the sound
of republican drums and seen their flags unfurled.

Keats Tweets

'Or like stout Cortez when with eagle eyes
He star'd at the Pacific—and all his men
Look'd at each other with a wild surmise—
Silent, upon a peak in Darien.'

A severed head* replies:
Fake news! Balboa was the first to see
what then was called the Southern Sea.
Forget those nineteenth-century tweets
by England's simpleton John Keats!
Besides, it's clear he'd never been
to Spain. If he had, he would've seen
that no Spaniard can be *silent* anywhere!
And Hernán Cortés was never there!
He hints that 'Balboa' doesn't scan,
that's why he used the other man.
But Núñez de Balboa's name
is not too long to fit the frame.
So, it's time to end this poetic coup
by giving the right conquistador his due:
I was the one who saw the new-found sea
from Darien. Not 'stout Cortés', but *me*!

(On behalf of Vasco Núñez de Balboa)

* Vasco Núñez de Balboa (1475-1519)
In 1513, while leading an expedition in search of gold, Balboa
sighted the Pacific Ocean. He claimed the ocean and all of its
shores for Spain, opening the way for later Spanish exploration

and conquest along the western coast of South America. Balboa's achievement and ambition posed a threat to Pedro Arias Dávila, the Spanish governor of Darién, who falsely accused him of treason and had him beheaded in early 1519.

Appointment at 10:30pm
Firing Squad

It's not the usual time for appointments of this kind.
The normal time is dawn but bastard Falangists
are happy to kill opponents when and where
they can. It's dark by 10:30 in August. Perfect
for murdering anarchists like me, Arcollas
Cabezas, banderillero, Galadí Melgar and
teachers like Galindo González, poets like Lorca.
We died together riddled with bullets and buried
heaven knows where. No-one cares, it seems
except, perhaps, Galindo's surviving family.
The Lorcas hope Federico's body's never found.

Epitaph for José Antonio Rivas Carballés

Some handmade boots have silently revealed
a secret, entombed since the Spanish Civil War
and if they could talk, I presume they'd say:

"José Antonio wore us every day, no matter
what the weather and we survived until today
thanks to the quality of our calfskin leather.
Our owner's blood was shed in Galicia
by a fascist militia in September 1936
and the mud from the unmarked grave
where we were interred still clings to us.
Unearthed in 2010, we knew the bones
of his feet were still inside us. We were
the bearers of a secret testimony
against the perpetrators of the crime:
Falangists who'd murdered the wearer
because he was a well-read libertarian,
a dangerous Red. All that interested the fascists
was that he was dead and the "ruling class"
had shown who was boss. Once we were exhumed,
someone learnt that José's children, Lenin, and Equality,
had had their names changed to reflect preferences
no doubt more to the liking of the authorities,
who despised frivolity. Equality was baptised
María Digna and Lenin became Ramiro,
the girl turned into a Catholic and the boy,
a Nationalist. María Digna, an avocation
of the Virgin, Ramiro after a Falangist
hero-martyr, murdered by Red Internationalists.

In 1936, youngsters didn't realize the Church
and Falange were in cahoots to kill Lenin's father,
but seventy-four years later, now octogenarians,
they claimed to remember his calfskin boots!
You will have guessed that our survival helped
José Antonio's remains to be finally laid to rest."

Time Traveller

The autumn of nineteen-fifty-seven
saw an eager young student set off for Spain,
an epic journey by train from a liberal
democracy that "had never had it so good",
to an autarkic dictatorship under Franco.

The young man's destination was Salamanca.
The imagination of this naive young man
had been stirred by a nineteenth-century poem,
The Student of Salamanca, a spellbinding,
Gothic reworking of the Don Juan theme
set in the city that possessed the oldest seat
of learning in the Hispanic world.

At Irun, he climbed aboard the antique
steam train that was to chug and rattle
its way across the bleak, windswept
landscape of Old Castile and León,
each stark kilometre taking him further
and further back in time!

The slatted wooden seats
of the third class carriage
mortified the flesh of the passengers,
almost entirely swarthy farm workers
clad in shabby brown corduroy.
The one nearest the student politely
offered to share his meal with him,
but he also expected his invitation

to be equally graciously refused
to complete the time-honoured ritual.

The train eventually arrived
on the outskirts of Salamanca
just as dawn was breaking.
The platform undulated eerily
in the half-light...until his eyes
adjusted to the gloom. The rippling
movement was caused by a dozen
harvesters wearing broadbrimmed
straw hats, squatting on their haunches,
wrapped in blankets and clutching sickles
wearily getting to their feet to board the train
to Zamora and its rolling wheatfields.

Even in those grey days of Franco,
the monumental city was still captivating
despite the asphyxiating male-dominated society.
After the evening meal, 'decent' women were seen out
only if chaperoned by a man from their family.
Relations between the sexes were closely monitored.
The ritual pre-lunch and pre-dinner paseos, or strolls,
around the main square that took place every day
were as elaborately choreographed as any ballet,
with the girls walking one way, arm-in-arm,
while the young men, coats draped on their shoulders,
strutted past in the other direction shouting *'piropos'*.
The girls would toss their heads in mock scorn
or boost the male egos with complicit smiles.
But no touching was allowed. At the appointed
hour everyone would go home to eat.

The Catholic Church held sway over family life.
During the day, its presence was visible everywhere.
At night, the streets were policed by a nightwatchman,
a 'sereno', armed with a truncheon and a whistle.
On his rounds, he would periodically call out the time
and declare that 'all was well', that is, *'sereno'*,
hence the name. He held the keys to the main door
of every building on his round. Late revellers
would have to call for the 'sereno' to open the door
of the hostel or guesthouse where they were staying,
and he would follow them in, to make sure
each went to his own room and nobody else's...

As a young man from the Perfidious Albion
the student remained under close surveillance
by the suspicious acolytes of the authorities...
His roommate was a Falangist Blue Shirt.

Putin on the Blitz

"If you're blue, and don't know what to do
why not go and give Ukraine the shits?"
Putin on the blitz.

"Different types of greatcoat, perfect fits,"
Putin on the blitz.

"Dressed up like a million-rouble trooper,
trying hard to be a party pooper.
Come, let's mix where sticks
of dynamite blow Ukraine to bits,"
Putin on the blitz.

Have you seen our Russian bane,
parading up and down Park Lane?
While being London's owners,
they're also Tory party donors,
slimy rats with arrow collars,
funding Putin's spats with lots of dollars.

Spending like there's no tomorrow,
they have no time for sorrow
for Ukrainians, who get *their* kicks
delivered by the blitz.
People die as missiles whine,
thanks to hateful Russian swine.

The world doesn't have to move
and groove

to Putin's botoxed biorhythms.
Where are the high-tech algorithms
to interfere with his communications
and frustrate his machinations?
Let's have peace in Ukraine and usher
in regime change in Mother Russia

Screenshot

Children are screaming, their mothers are weeping
as they pick their way slowly over the rubble
of what used to be Mariupol.
Unburdened by luggage but weighed down with anxiety,
they scramble to safety
through streets strewn with sadness.
Hemmed in by havoc, pale faces, red-eyed with tears,
transmit their fears to us
safe at home watching the news.

Picture Post...Mortem

Watching reports of the war on TV,
viewers are horror-struck to see
a frantic mother, howling in despair
while a pair of paramedics try to save
the life of her shrapnel-wounded baby.
Maybe, just maybe they can… but they can't.
The maternity hospital was not bombed in error,
it was a deliberate act of Russian terror.
Next, the camera shows another young mother,
face blank, hair lank, flopped on the floor
of a hospital corridor.
She's clutching her child that survived the air raid.
Stunned, in shock, she's silently crying
because her other two children
are presently lying dead in their beds.

Moscow

Fall friendly bombs on dread Moscow
much more deserving than poor Slough.
Stand up, Putin; take a bow,
Meet your fate, Death!

You must get your just deserts,
especially if it really hurts,
both you and your grim perverts.
Gasp your last breath!

Destroy the city and the thug
who sits at that table looking smug
as he sets out to pull the plug
on all mankind.

Don't forget Lavrov whose droopy features
reveal the most cynical of creatures.
Oh, he's a credit to his teachers:
Evil defined.

And smash Russia Today (not tomorrow)
And smash those who are spreading sorrow.
Let's see them all light up like flambeaux.
Burn, baby, burn!

And don't spare the oligarchs who add
to the profits of the repulsive Vlad.
They are greedy rather than mad.
Some never learn.

They can't pretend they didn't know
Vlad's grand plan. It's only the dough
that interests them, going with the flow.
Send them to Hell!

Each one's been delighted with his lot,
spending millions on a superyacht
while leaving compatriots to rot.
Hear their death knell.

Putin kills civilians by the score
in this criminal act of war.
He exudes venom from every pore.
It's payback time.

Fall friendly bombs on dread Moscow,
ensure it's no longer fit for plough.
Let nothing thrive there now.
And spread quicklime.

Home is not so Sad

At home, we're watching the news on TV.
Ukraine forces have recaptured Kherson,
now devastated, looted, and evacuated
by the Russians, who've crossed the Dnipro.
A Spanish television reporter follows
a sturdy Ukrainian man as he enters
a shell-shattered building: his home.
Visibly moved, he surveys the wreckage
of his modest house. We follow the eye
of the camera as it slowly pans around
showing us two of the walls still standing
while another offers a gaping hole
of the kind safecrackers might make
when breaking into the vault of a bank.
We viewers assume he's emotional
because of the damage done to his home,
yet his tears are welling up, he says,
not because of the state of the house
but because at last he's back home.

Russian Oligarchs
From Top Dogs to No-Marks

Russian oligarchs found out in 2022
that they had their very own Atropos:
the pint-sized Putin who'd outsourced
the snipping of threads to his minions,
some more imaginative than others.
Defenestrations were pretty popular
but always disguised as accidents
or suicides by the careless and depressed.
"Accident-prone" executives from
Gazprom and Lukoil were found to be
falling out of windows, and one over a cliff.
Putin's lethal reach can stretch beyond Russia,
so it's a waste of time for oligarchs to try
to imitate the runners of *Logan's Run*
for there is no sanctuary for anyone
who opposes Putin's appalling policies
and the cruel devastation of Ukraine.
Throughout last year, twenty-two former
wealthy "friends" of Putin met strange deaths,
all of whom had been his faithful yes-men.
Fickle Putin turned them into no-men.
After all, he did it *pour encourager les autres*
yet no one gives a kopek for their stand-ins either.
Even the editor-in-chief of Komsomoiskaya Pravda
had a stroke and suffocated on his way to lunch.
Who knows what caused it or who stroked him?
The editor's *pravda* did not match comrade Putin's,
that much was patently obvious to the analysts.

Was the editor's *pravda* polluting young Russian minds
instead of feeding them the Kremlin's propaganda?
The oligarchs now get the message loud and clear:
don't criticize and don't oppose. Putin rules by fear.

From Maggie to Maggots

The corruption giving off the stench
contaminates Parliament and the UK.
It mainly comes from the Tory front bench
in both the Commons and House of Lords.
The maggots gorging on a putrid cadaver
formed by the cabinet and Tory factions,
including the scruff who's all wind and blather,
are using their power to enrich themselves.
The blond buffoon who's telling us lies,
by far the fattest maggot of all,
is rotting before our very eyes.
Meanwhile, the fat cats lick the cream
and all the pigs are at the trough,
an endless line of pin-striped swine
whose snouts can never find enough to "scoff"
as copious "pigswill" flows galore.
It's taxpayers money that's being pocketed,
siphoned off by the crooks in power.
Just look how their donors' profits've rocketed.
Conservative maggots and worms in their hundreds
are asset-stripping the country bare
to fill the coffers of insatiable friends
and what is more, they do not care!
They're quite determined to centralize power
because democracy's not what matters.
Their aim is to boost a private chumocracy
while a once great nation lies in tatters.

A Country Member

Johnson is a country member,
whose wallet's in the shires,
which are desperate to dismember
the state for Johnson who aspires
to riches for himself and all his chums.
Tories are lower than vermin,
we'll be lucky to get the crumbs.
The Cons share out the ermine
to ensure their sinecures, OK?
Essential workers, just remember:
make sure you're ready for the fray,
because Johnson is a country member…

Acknowledgements

Embers published by Shoestring Press 2020 (UK)

Lithuanian Cat's Cradle published in Critical Survey (UK)

Chance Encounter (1990), Love's a Laugh and *Life on the Streets* and *Tailgating Time* published by London Grip New Poetry (UK)

Appointment at 10:30 (F Squad) and *Home is not so Sad* published by Pure Slush (Australia)

Rita, Solidarity and *Graffiti: Wall to Wall Wisdom* published by Cajun Mutt Press (USA),

Pater Noster and *Family Funerals* published in Otherwise Engaged Vol 10

Octave for Janet published by Quilled Ink Review

In a Rut and *Holy Man or Homeless Man* published by Impspired

Attempted Suicide, Joan of Arc, Case Closed, Dead to Rights, Memory, The Six-Shooter, The Worm in the Rose and *Putin on the Blitz* published by The Five-Two (USA)

Maradona Meets His Maker, Online Poetry Magazines, Ferlinghetti Tribute I am waiting, Sights and Sounds, Fade to Black and *End of a Reign* published as recordings in The Syndic Literary Journal (USA)

Hidden Meanings, published by poetryandcovid, (UK)

The Country Member and *From Maggie to Maggots* published by Loch Raven Review (USA)

Moscow published by Beatnik Cowboy

Screenshot and *Picture Post....Mortem* published by North of Oxford (USA)

An App for Ancient Swingers published by Home Planet News
Poetry by Design and *Prudence* published by Lighten Up Online
LA Christmas Present published by Retreats from Oblivion
End Times published in Our Changing Earth Vol 1
Time Traveller published by Exit 13